From Pain to Promise:
Discovering Your Purposeful Wait!

Rebecca   P.   Rush

From Pain to Promise: Discovering your Purposeful Wait Copyright© December 2013 by Rebecca P. Rush

Published in the United States of America by Gospel 4 U Publishing

All rights reserved. No part of this book may be reproduced or transmitted in anyway by means, electronic, mechanical, Photocopy, recording or otherwise, without prior permission of the author except as provided by USA copyright law.

Scriptures are taken from the King James Version unless otherwise marked.
ISBN 978-0-9896249-9-2
Printed in United States of America
December 2013

Contents

FOREWORD

ACKNOWLEDGEMENTS

DEDICATION

The Need to Suffer..1

The Trial Begins 5

Obsession: Is God My Desire?......................................13

A Great Disappointment..17

The Stupid Place..25

A Leap of Faith..29

A Birthing Season..35

Purposeful Wait..41

The Battlefield 47

Release: The Vault Is Opened.......................................53

Twice the Test..59

Arrival of the Verdict 69

A Peace of Faith 73

Purposeful Wait Precepts 79

Rejoicing with Others vs. Jealousy 81

Thankfulness vs. Complaining 87

Faith vs. Fear 91

Peace vs. Worry 95

Patience vs. Hastiness 99

Courage vs. Despair 103

Persistence vs. Unfaithfulness 107

REBECCA P. RUSH

Foreword

As Rebecca's mom, I have had the pleasure of seeing Rebecca mature as she took hold of the truths of Christ and the Gospel. But there is no greater joy as a mom than to see your child take hold of the power that lies behind these truths, and use them as a weapon to destroy yokes of bondage in her own life, as well as the lives of others. Many will be inspired to hold on, as they read this up close and frank account of tests, trials, and triumphs on the way to purpose.

There is much to take in as Rebecca attests to how powerfully God's Word worked to change her feelings and attitudes. She makes a very strong case for the doubter to see that "… all things work together for good to them that love God, to them who are the called according to His purpose". (Romans 8:28 KJV).

From Pain to Promise: Discovering your Purposeful Wait will motivate readers to discover their own purpose in the midst of their trials, even as the author discovered her own purpose. Her memoirs from her waiting period during a major trial make it quite clear that God has called her to help others find purpose in their waiting period.

Throughout the entire book relevant scripture verses are presented. The author implies that they have the power to change your life, even as they have changed her life through meditation and application to situations.

At the end of the book the author shares seven Purposeful Wait Precepts or principles which the Lord taught her during her time of testing. She expounds on each one with definitions, descriptions, examples and of course, scripture. These can be used as a teaching tool, or simply as guidelines to discern if you are purposefully waiting. Whether your waiting period turns out to be short, or even as long as twenty years, this book will help you gain the courage to find purpose as you wait.

Maria R. Palmer

Pastor, Mother and Friend

Acknowledgements

I would first like to give all glory and honor to my Lord and Savior Jesus Christ, who is the very reason for my existence. I know that I could have never made it without Him, and for that I am very grateful.

Lord, I owe you my all and I thank you for strengthening me throughout this process; so much that I was able to write this book. You are my true inspiration and motivation in life itself!

To my wonderful husband Fred, I thank you for supporting me in all my endeavors. You are my best friend, the one who drives me to go after more in life, as well as the one who accepts me for who I am. Thank you for standing by me during this process…I love you!

To my parents, Mom and Dad, I just can't say enough. Your support and overall love for me is amazing! You two are such Godly examples that I thank the Lord for often. I could not have asked for better parents, and I thank God for the role you both play in my life. Not only are you my earthly parents, but my spiritual parents as well. God set that up so perfectly! Thank you for believing in me and praying me through! Mom, thank you for using your gifts to edit this book and write the foreword.

To my sister Rachel, I praise God for the friendship and loving relationship we share. Your spirit is so sweet and inspiring even throughout our years growing up with one another. I thank God for your support and love that is evident and so much needed. You are a well- trusted friend and I cherish our relationship very much. To my brother Joshua, I love you so much! Thank you for your encouraging words and genuine acceptance of me. I can't wait to experience the ministry that God births in you as you walk in His calling!

To Pastor Joanna, my friend, prayer partner, and publisher…thank you! I am so grateful for the friendship we share and the Godly influence you have been in my life. You have been so supportive of me through good times and testing times. God has proved you to be a trusted friend, and for that I thank you!

Finally, to all of my friends thank you so much for your support and prayers over the years. I thank God for you all and your encouraging words. It truly has meant a lot to me. You all have a very special place in my heart.

Dedication

I dedicate this book to my two little angels that I never met. From the moment I learned of you, I loved you. I tried to keep you safe for as long as I could, but God had a bigger purpose for you in heaven. I know you both are resting in the arms of the almighty so there is no doubt that you are safe. I pray that one day I will see you again. *"Before I formed thee in the belly I knew thee; and before thou camest forth out of the womb I sanctified thee, and I ordained thee a prophet unto the nations."* ~ **Jeremiah 1:5**

The Need to Suffer

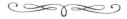

Whenever I would think about suffering I always imagined having trials in my life, but nothing really that serious. Truth be told, who wants to ponder what type of problems they will face in this life? Not me! However, suffering is important for believers, and if I consider myself to be a born again Christian then I too must face some giants. The Bible says in **1 Peter 4:12-13** *"12 Beloved, think it not strange concerning the fiery trial which is to try you, as though some strange thing happened unto you: 13 But rejoice, inasmuch as ye are partakers of Christ's sufferings; that, when his glory shall be revealed, ye may be glad also with exceeding joy."*

This text implies the necessity of suffering for Christ's sake. So whenever we encounter a trial, we are to endure it, knowing that we are not alone in this race.

It is interesting how trials sometimes come as a testing from the Lord. If you are anything like me you are aware that these trials often bring us closer to God. You might think how is that? Well for me, having a consistent problem or burden has always led me to pray more often than I usually do. This tendency is not exactly how I would want it, but if I am totally honest with myself then I realize this thought is in fact true.

It's hard to swallow when our suffering comes from our pure act of disobedience. At times God is calling us to greater, and He wants us to move forward with the vision and dream that He has given us. So what do we do? We procrastinate and ignore the urgency that the Lord has placed in our hearts to fulfill that plan. It often takes a fiery trial or test to finally snap us out of that frame of mind and bring us on our knees for some true seeking. I know for myself at one point I was so self absorbed. I knew that God had placed ministry in my heart and I truly had a heart to serve. Every time I was ready to go full speed ahead, it almost felt like I would hit a premature speed bump that slowed me down and caused me to yield to my own problems and issues. It wasn't until God finally brought me to a place where the only wise door out was through service to Him and His kingdom that I yielded; hence the trial began.

The Trial Begins

I remember so clearly sitting beside my husband in church one day when we had a guest speaker during a revival. The speaker was a familiar face and always ministered to many when she came to my church, Brand New Life Christian Center in Philadelphia. She is known for her prophecies that are accurately spoken from the Lord. Well this particular day my husband and I were listening to the message when the speaker turned to us and said, "Are you two planning to have a child?" My eyes widened and I am assuming I had a puzzled look on my face because to my knowledge we were not planning at the time! Nonetheless, I looked at my husband and a little frightened, attempted to display a smile. She then said to us, "Well I see that...I see it happening." I stared at her anxiously thinking I wonder when. After she saw our response, she quickly continued on with her message.

Literally three weeks later I started feeling

extremely fatigued and tired. I was still in graduate school and working my internship for most of the week. I can remember being at the site and literally fighting to stay awake. I must say it was truly a battle. I had to encounter clients and talk with them for quite some time, and was embarrassed when I found my eyelids seemingly becoming heavier. One day I recall thinking something is just not right. Thoughts ruminated in my mind about being out of shape to the point that I needed to lose some weight. While this may have been true, another thought quickly intruded my mind…I wonder if I could be pregnant? The more I thought about this latter idea, the more I reminisced on the moment the Prophetess spoke to my husband Fred and I about planning for a child. I quickly began to run with this notion and started researching signs and symptoms on the internet. To my amazement, it seemed like I was experiencing many of the so called "early pregnancy signs," that is except one of the major ones, morning sickness.

After several days of Google searches, I finally decided to purchase a pregnancy test. I rushed home to take it and anxiously awaited the results thinking *what if*

I really am? When the three minute wait period ended I quickly glanced at the test and interpreted the results…NOT PREGNANT. Although I was somewhat relieved to read that statement I was also a little disappointed.

Two more weeks had passed and I realized my monthly visitor had not showed up as usual. I remembered that the home pregnancy test I purchased had two urine tests in the package, which meant there was one more left. The next day I woke up thinking, let me just take this test to rule out the possibility of being pregnant. In my heart I truly doubted that I was expecting a child, but in the back of my mind I wanted to be. Nonetheless I rushed to the bathroom and prayed as I allowed the test to do its work. Two minutes later I picked up the stick to read…PREGNANT! I must have blinked my eyes about ten times before it finally sunk in…I AM PREGNANT! The tear ducts in my eyes flooded with tears of excitement and nervousness, as I covered my mouth and said "Oh my God…it's true!"

A few days passed until my visit to the doctor in

order to confirm my pregnancy. As my husband and I met with the doctor she took another urine test, then congratulated us and talked about what our next steps should be. I eagerly asked the doctor to calculate my due date and was ecstatic when she replied February 1, 2013. I screamed... "That's my mother's birthday!" As I began to allow the excitement to flow I had blood drawn so they could verify that this was a healthy pregnancy. A few days later I received a phone call from the doctor's office confirming I was in my sixth week of pregnancy with our first child!

It was all finally beginning to sink in. Fred and I had returned home from church one Sunday afternoon and were sitting in our living room eating our normal Sunday after church snack. I suddenly had an urge to use the bathroom and was puzzled at what I saw. I was bleeding, and heavily. I quickly cleaned myself up and ran into the dining room to tell Fred. He calmly suggested that we call the doctor. I remember speaking with the on-call doctor who informed me to stay calm and told me what to watch out for, like heavy cramps, and abdominal pain. He then recommended that we call first thing the next morning and schedule an emergency appointment to be seen by one of the obstetricians. Well, the bleeding continued throughout the night and the following day. In the morning I called as the doctor advised, and scheduled an appointment for later that afternoon. Fred had agreed to accompany me to the doctor, and we went together hoping for the best care and best report. We had been praying that our child was fine, and that this was simply my body still responding to the many changes during pregnancy. When we arrived at the doctor's office we met with one of the female doctors at the practice who was very friendly and personable. She was empathetic and explained everything she needed to do in order to make sure the pregnancy was not at risk. She took several tests and ordered an ultrasound to ensure the baby was developing like he or she needed to.

The next week entailed nothing but several trips back and forth to the doctor's office, and lab to have blood work done. After receiving an ultrasound and being called back to the doctor to review all of the findings, they finally said it. The doctor very calmly said "I think you are having an early miscarriage and it is proved by your dropping HCG levels. Do you have any questions?" I allowed it to sink in for a few seconds, then attempted to clear my throat after the news triggered a dissatisfying taste in my mouth. Is he serious? I thought to myself. I could not believe he just told me that news so nonchalantly, then asked if I had any questions. I finally replied, " No".

The next few weeks which eventually led to months, were the most trying for me. I could not believe that God had blessed my womb, only to allow my child to be lost and swallowed up. I honestly felt like I was being punished for something I did not even know I did. I was hurting, and nothing anyone could say or do would help at the time. I prayed and cried, then prayed and cried, then prayed and cried, until I thought my body cannot possibly give up so many tears…sooner or later I would be dehydrated from all the water loss. My husband even tried to comfort me; which lasted for a while, but I was still in pain.

The emotional rollercoaster was in fact hard to keep up with. Some days I would be totally fine. I would go to class or my internship and go throughout my day as if nothing happened at all. I loved those days! They were what felt like at the time, God sent! However, those days were not every day. Sometimes I would struggle to get myself out of bed and get before the throne of grace. It was difficult at times to even open up my mouth and pray. That's how bad my problem was beginning to take over my life! I wanted out! Out of this situation, but at the time I just did not know how.

Obsession: Is God My Desire?

It was early October of 2012 when I truly started to worry...what's wrong with me? Why was I not getting pregnant again? Why was it taking so long now that my husband and I were actually trying? I made several attempts to analyze the problem in my mind, but regardless of what methods I used it was just not making any sense. I mean, I had prayed for four months now so what could possibly be the reasons for my delay? These were amongst the many questions I was beginning to ask God in my prayer closet. I could not comprehend why what I thought should have been so easy and natural, was now seemingly a struggle and constant fight. In my mind, it did not make any sense whatsoever.

There were nights when I would spend hours on Google search viewing women's testimonials of waiting to conceive and the journey they encountered. Sometimes these stories would give me hope, while at other times they were simply discouraging. In spite of what I found, I continued to read all about pregnancy day and night. I had gone beyond the point of interest all the way to the idea of obsession. Yes I said it…OBSESSION! The humorous part about this is that during the wait, it never felt like obsession. In my heart I had convinced myself that I was just investing in knowledge and learning more about motherhood. Though I had deceived myself, God knew my heart! In spite of it all He never let go of me!

Day after day my researching continued. Only this time my thoughts began to follow my findings. Whatever I learned about on the internet, I thought deeply about it and pondered on it for quite some time. At this point I knew my deep desire to bear a child/children was crossing over to idolatry. I was spending more time on the internet and thinking about having a baby, than I was with my Heavenly Father. If you know the God I serve, then you will agree that God was not having that! When there is a calling on your life, a person can spend but so much time doing other things besides seeking the face of God. In my frustration I finally realized that this obsession was getting the best of me. It was draining my emotions, energy, time, and spirituality. Yes, this constant concern with the desire to be pregnant now was controlling my entire life. There was not one day that would go by that I would not think about having a baby.

It seemed as though out of nowhere everyone and their friend, cousin, or even mother was having a child. Everyone but me! "Why was God torturing me like this?", I often thought to myself. My lack of understanding would not allow me to be completely happy for other women who were pregnant. I just could not fathom why the Lord allowed His faithful one (so I thought) to wait and endure so much pain while others were getting pregnant left and right. It was an unfortunate feeling to live with, and I would not wish it on my worst enemy!

It became even worse! No matter how much I prayed and meditated and worshiped, I just could not see past my pain. The reality of my now, was seemingly taking over my future. How? Because I was so caught up in the past, that I was not allowing God to take me into my purpose; I was still holding on when God had already instructed me to let go. "When was God going to just give me my desire?" I had this thought day after day, until one day the Lord rebuked me during my quiet time with Him. He revealed to me that my first desire needed to be Him. If my first desire was not the Lord, then anything else I believed Him for, would not come with haste. Instead, it would tarry, until I finally return to my first love-Jesus Christ.

When our desire to receive the promise of the Lord is greater than receiving the love of God, something's wrong. Well, that's where I was at the time; a mindset that can be called, "the stupid place."

A Great Disappointment

In January of 2013 the year had just began and my biggest wish to the Lord was for Him to bless my womb with children. I was not caught up in all these New Year's resolutions. I knew that it was easy for me to speak of goals and plans, however it is much harder to follow through. Moreover, I decided to continue praying and seeking the Lord for the one thing that I had no control over. A few days into the month I had expected my monthly visitor to come as it normally would during that time of my cycle. Instead it delayed. After being a few days late I decided to take a pregnancy test. I just remember being so anxious as I was waiting for the results to appear.

I thought to myself "it's probably positive, cause I've waited so long for this!" To my surprise it was negative! Can you believe that? I immediately allowed my emotions to get the best of me and disappointment began to set in. I just did not understand why something so simple had to be such a hurdle for me. It almost felt like everyone else had to walk around the track while I had to run cross country while jumping over constant hurdles. These are the types of analogies that would flood my mind after unexpected results.

Nonetheless, I went back to my normal routine of work and would count the days when my period never showed up. Finally it had been a whole week and I decided to take another test. NEGATIVE! I would laugh at the results for a few minutes, and then cry ten minutes later once the unfortunate news sunk in. I was tired of this emotional rollercoaster, but little did I know I would be taking that ride numerous times throughout the next three months.

Week after week I took a trip into the drug store to purchase more pregnancy tests, since surely one of these tests will prove I am carrying a child! Every time I was ready to actually take the test I would pray first, and then move forward with what developed into a routine. The more false results I received, the more my faith level began to rise. Yes, despite the several negative tests, I still believed in my heart that eventually it would test positive. I returned to my old ways with spending countless time on Google researching past stories of women who tested positive for pregnancy two and three months later. After reading many stories of miracles occurring after women were told no, I sought the doctor.

As clear as day the nurse told me, "there's no way possible that you are pregnant if the urine test said no." I would huff and puff on the line and ask if the doctor would see me anyway. After several attempts to be seen, they finally scheduled me for an appointment to come in and have a consultation with the doctor.

Before attending my doctor's appointment I would pray and ask God to place me in the right hands of people who would listen to me and be optimistic about the situation. In other words, I was tired of talking with nurses and receptionists who were boldly negative regardless of what story I told them. It was time for someone to hear my story and have faith in what I was telling them. After all, my body was changing and I was experiencing minor symptoms of pregnancy. My breasts were becoming fuller, my lower back was aching, I was spotting, and my belly was bloated. How could these doctors explain all of this along with a missed period!

The appointment with my doctor went exceptionally well even though I did not receive any positive news at the time. At least everyone I encountered at the office had a positive outlook on my situation. No one told me there was no way I was pregnant; that is what I wanted to hear! My doctor asked me, "You would like to be pregnant wouldn't you?" "Of course" I responded. Following the appointment I was scheduled for an ultrasound and to have blood drawn, as I had hoped for. My doctor believed that the symptoms could be a result of a small cyst that was found on my left ovary after my first pregnancy. Regardless of what her reasons were, I was happy that at least the blood work and ultrasound would reveal what I had been praying for the last eight months.

Throughout the course of three and a half months I was without a period, I often sought the Lord for understanding and peace. I remember reading various stories and parables in the Bible about people healed through their faith. This concept stayed with me day after day. It encouraged me to know that the God that I serve is able to do anything, and will grant certain things according to our faith and trust in Him.

The day before my ultrasound was a Sunday. After receiving a good word and some prayer from one of the ministers at church, I was feeling hopeful. I went home to relax with my husband and get prepared for the next day. To my surprise, I noticed I was spotting when I went to use the bathroom. Although I was quite confused about what I saw, I quickly reviewed some scriptures regarding faith. Regardless of what I saw I knew in my heart that my child was on the way. That's how elevated my faith was at the time. My faith was beyond the size of a mustard seed so all I needed to do was speak it into existence!

Monday arrived and it was a pleasant day throughout the morning and afternoon. Work did not hinder my move of faith because my miracle was soon to be exposed. The evening slowly came and I was excited to attend my appointment. I made sure to drink the 32 ounces of water required for the pelvic ultrasound. After registering for my ultrasound at the hospital, I eagerly sat in the waiting room as the water traveled through my body triggering my urge to use the bathroom. As inhales and exhales left my body, I continued to breathe at ease as I waited. A soft voice then interrupted my concentration as the technician called my name. Finally! I jumped up so quickly and walked back with my husband to the room.

    Laying on my back and feeling the cold gel cover my abdomen, I quickly prayed, "Okay God, this is it!" Patiently waiting for the technician to reveal what was in my womb, I smiled and breathed very slowly. A few minutes had passed and the tech continued to move the object back and forth on my lower abdomen, taking pictures of what was inside. This is when fear began to creep in. I began to get worried. Why wasn't she showing me the screen yet? Why is she taking so many pictures? Is something wrong? All of these questions flooded my mind as I lay stiff on my back. The technician then proceeded to tell me I could get dressed and use the bathroom in order to empty my full bladder. I was anxious, yet relieved. Approximately four minutes later I was back in the room and preparing for a vaginal ultrasound. Again, the tech moved the camera back and forth only this time it was inside of me. An uneasy feeling even though I understood why this procedure was done. Towards the end I nervously inquired about the ultrasound and what was found. The tech responded, "The doctor will review the results and follow through with an outcome." Even though I was not pleased with her response, I answered, "Okay, thank you."

During the next day, I received a phone call from my doctor's office with the results from the ultrasound. I eagerly listened as my heartbeat intensified. The nurse told me, "Your ultrasound revealed that everything is fine. The cyst on your left ovary is the same as it was before, so it has not grown. Your uterus is normal with no issues." She then asked me to follow up with an appointment to talk with the doctor within the next few days. As I hung up the phone the tear ducts in my eyes quickly filled up. The tears began to fall and did not ease up anytime soon. I could not believe it! I waited three and a half months to hear the doctor say I was not pregnant. Unbelievable I thought. How could God allow me to endure all of these changes, only to hear that it was all for nothing?

The Stupid Place

It did not take long for discouragement to sink in. To be exact, it took approximately 5 minutes. I was in shock almost to the point where I felt numb. This entire experience was just meaningless! I struggled to maintain any form of positive attitude throughout all of this. I could not fathom why God would allow this in my life. For what! I could not wait to see my husband. I was going to vent about the pointless situation to him all night! At least that's what I thought was going to happen; a part of me wanted things to go that way. I wanted a pity party.

My husband arrived home from being at work all day. He found me in the bed lying underneath the covers. He immediately asked me why I was in the bed at such an early hour. I did not hesitate to pour out all of my feelings about what happened. I told Fred about the unfortunate news and phone call I received earlier that day. Although he was not happy to hear the news, he did not join my pity party-otherwise known as "the stupid place." "What's the point of Him putting me through all of this if He's not going to get any glory out of it? This is dumb!" I yelled. "I'm not going to church tonight either...for what!" I cried aloud hysterically for a few seconds until Fred finally interrupted me. He told me that he was surprised to even hear me talk like that about God. Fred reminded me that if I were to keep that negative attitude, things would never change. So I wiped my eyes with the back of my hand and sat there with a dull expression on my face. The truth is he was right. I was just hurting so bad that I allowed my emotions to take control, which resulted in some disrespectful talk to my Heavenly Father. The Holy Spirit immediately convicted me, right in the middle of my negative talk and attitude. I was wrong and despite the amount of disappointment I felt, my approach to the Lord was incorrect. God used Fred that day to rebuke me in love. Sometimes a real friend is needed during the stupid place, because they will challenge you to repent and get away from the negativity.

Furthermore, what is this stupid place I

encountered? The stupid place is a point in your waiting season where you find yourself in self-pity and defeat. In fact, you are not actually defeated but you feel that way because of your discouragement, impatience, and discontentment. I recall staying in this place for quite some time. I was so miserable with my situation that I became angry-angry with God for allowing me to even experience such an embarrassing and shameful matter. Often as believers we enter into a period in our lives when we feel tempted to become hopeless, and discouraged. Although we do not wish to stay in that place, we often remain there because of our lack of faith and belief in the power of God. We say we have faith that God is going to do whatever He has promised, but when it comes to waiting we become allergic to waiting and are ready to throw in the towel after one week of testing. God had to show me that one week, and even one month in my case was not going to develop perseverance.

Remember, perseverance must have its work within us so that we are mature and complete, lacking nothing (see **James 1:4 NIV**). Instead God allowed me to wait month after month, in order to help me establish some patience. The tribulation helped to develop more patience. Sooner or later I had to take myself out of that "Stupid Place" if I wanted to move on with my life. That's right...you can remove yourself from the "Stupid Place." However, you cannot handle it in your own strength. It takes the power of the Holy Spirit to comfort and deliver you from the discouraged mindset. This does not mean that you can automatically leave the valley experience that God has allowed you to be in, but your perspective and outlook on the entire situation will in fact change. So in other words, He will give you the peace of God which transcends all understanding (see **Philippians 4:7 NIV**).

A Leap of Faith

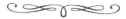

After my great disappointment and "Stupid Place" experience I finally realized that God was trying to speak to me, but I was so preoccupied that I did not hear the message. Now was the time for me to shut everything down, and listen for that still small voice. Although it took me quite some time to recognize that I needed the Holy Spirit to help me get out of the "Stupid Place," it was not a long process to cast down that defeated mind frame.

Before my great disappointment I had rid myself of most of my major distractions which at the time were Facebook, Instagram, and television. I can remember logging on to Facebook and checking my news feed. Well what was supposed to be only 15 minutes or so, ended up to be an hour and then two hours. I would spend all of that time looking at other peoples' statuses and pictures. It even appeared as though every time I logged on, I would find someone new who was expecting a child. Every time I noticed someone else was having a baby, it only reminded me of my situation and burning desire to have children.

Enough was enough! I disabled my Facebook account and stopped watching television. During the normal hours that I would browse the internet or watch television, I began to read my Word more; studying and meditating on His promises. Things truly began to make more sense and I could hear God's voice so clearly. In order to consistently hear that still small voice, there has to be no distractions. If a person is constantly listening to other people or even their own words, how will they ever be able to tune in to the voice of God? Throughout the time when I would rest and be still before the Lord, He gave me so many visions.

For example, one day I was driving with my coworker during work hours. We were in an industrial area when we suddenly saw a herd of deer standing together. As we talked about the strangeness of this sight, we drove five minutes further and noticed another herd of deer! My coworker laughed about the weirdness in what we had witnessed. It was approximately four o'clock in the afternoon when we saw this. As eager as I was to laugh too, something within me was so curious about the deer.

Later that evening, the Holy Spirit reminded me of the sight I encountered earlier. I quickly prayed then looked up the biblical meaning of deer. To my amazement, I came across these two scriptures: *"The LORD God is my strength, and he will make my feet like hinds' feet, and he will make me to walk upon mine high places. To the chief singer on my stringed instruments"* **Habakkuk 3:19.** *"He maketh my feet like hinds' feet, and setteth me upon my high places"* **Psalm 18:33.** The NIV translation replaces hinds with deer. After completing more research about deer in general, the Lord gave me a revelation. He showed me that He allowed me to see the deer because they were symbolic of the changes He is doing in my life. Deer are able to climb to higher heights often because they keep their focus above and fail to look down because fear will set in and ruin them climbing higher. Just like the deer the Lord was bringing me to higher heights with my faith and trust in Him, however in order to stay focused and be able to successfully proceed to the next level, I will need to maintain my focus on God and His Word. Once the Lord revealed this to me I was excited that He took the time to send those deer to that location at the specific time for me to see them. To know that God did that just for me was encouraging. God is faithful!

The vision of a camel quickly came to my mind one day as I rested in my home. I knew it was no ordinary vision there was something uniquely special about this animal. Seeking the Lord first I asked about a camel. Why did an instant picture of a camel flash in my thoughts suddenly? This is the question I asked the Lord. I spent time researching this interesting animal, which is not commonly mentioned in today's world. Suddenly the Lord revealed to me its significance in my life. The camel was symbolic of a journey. Furthermore, a camel is a reliable animal that is often used to travel long periods of time from one destination to another. Camels are known for their long travels. They are able to endure a long journey without water, and are considered to be animals that can carry or bear things. God opened up my understanding by showing me that I am like the camel in a sense. He has equipped me to undergo the journey of waiting however long it may be. Even though at times the journey may seem too long and unbearable, God has already given me the strength I will need to make it to my destination.

Often God directs us to witness or see different things that are symbolic of our spiritual journey. In fact, many times we may believe that we happened to come across certain things when God is truly trying to reveal something significant to us. However, we must be careful. If we are not tuned in to the voice of God and sensitive to the Holy Spirit, we will miss our word. There is no such thing as a coincidence in a child of God's life!

A Birthing Season

A few months prior the Lord had connected me with a woman who I had so much in common with. Not only was she a woman of God, but she experienced the same testing that I did. She persevered and now has a beautiful one year old daughter, as well as another child on the way. Look at God!

Moreover, as time progressed I realized why the Lord connected me with her at that specific time. Interestingly, I already knew her but did not develop a relationship with her until my birthing season. A family member of hers informed me of a ministry she began called "Faith Walk." The ministry entails woman gathering together once a month on an early Saturday morning to pray together, and then walk around the track by faith. Through her prayers and encouragement I began to walk by faith too-that is around the track. The ministry had so many examples of people who believed God for something, and experienced God's supernatural power during their involvement with Faith Walk. It inspired me so much to trust God and find His Godly ordained purpose for my life.

The clock continued to tick as the days and weeks passed. Even though I felt stronger in my waiting season, I was still wondering when my prayers would finally be answered. I would consistently vent to my Godsent friend during those times when I would feel the heat from the fiery trial. Every month it seemed like I heard the news from someone different that they were with child. Although the grace of God had allowed me to rejoice with them, it always triggered my pondering on my own situation. When was I going to be able to share my wonderful news that Fred and I were expecting? In my heart I had hoped that the news would come soon, however I had no idea and this notion always made me feel nervous. I remember hearing so many sermons and messages about God's timing and the "appointed time." I knew that God's time was perfect, but I also wanted His time to be now! Often times I would beg God and actually envision myself as a kid in the candy store pulling on their father's arm for candy (yes it was that bad). There was not a single day that went by where I did not think about having children. It was my heart's desire and something so valuable to me that I would never give up on it. God had already given me several visions and dreams of me pregnant, and one specific vision of my child's face. I recall one day resting in my bed when the Lord gave me a clear vision. I saw a woman holding an infant boy on her side. The woman's face was turned away, yet the boy was looking clearly at me. His face was so familiar even though I had never seen him before. He resembled my husband. It was then that I realized the woman was me, and the boy was my son. With tears I widely opened up my eyes realizing that it was not yet time for me to meet him.

Suddenly a sadness came over me. Why would God show me this if I could not see him now? It almost felt like a teaser, so I thought at the time. Then the Holy Spirit convicted me reminding me that visions are yet for the appointed time. *"For the vision is yet for an appointed time, but at the end it shall speak, and not lie: though it tarry, wait for it; because it will surely come, it will not tarry"* **Habakkuk 2:3**.

These experiences prompted me to pray earnestly. I needed God's continual peace if I was going to wait on Him. So I prayed and sought the face of God. I needed daily grace to have enough strength to continue trusting and believing God to do what He said He would do. I never once doubted that God would do it, I just did not know when. The longer my wait seemed to be, the more I prayed. My prayers began to shift from "Lord send me children," to "Lord help me to serve during my wait; not my will but your will be done."

Something was different now. I had learned that my life was truly not my own, so regardless of what problems I encountered God still had work for me to do. This mindset only came through prayer, reading the Bible, and worship. God began to show me exactly what to pray for. I had let go of the self-absorbed pity party mind frame and allowed God to show me how to serve through my pain. I sought the Lord to understand what my true purpose was during my wait. What did I need to be doing differently? How could God get the glory out of my testimony? I must have asked the Lord these questions numerous times before one day it finally began to make sense.

Purposeful Wait

During prayer and meditation on the Word of God, I heard the Lord say the words "Purposeful Wait." Although at the time I had no idea what I was supposed to do I knew the relevancy in the phrase. God began to show me that there is divine purpose in waiting. The more I wondered about the phrase, the more I prayed and asked God to reveal it to me. Well one day after sitting in an all day training for my job my mind began to tune into the term "Purposeful Wait." The topic of the training was geared to trauma and how it affects families and individuals in society. There was one particular portion of the training that highlighted the resiliency of those who find purpose in their experience with trauma which enables them to view their experience in a whole new light. This notion is what triggered my thinking about my own experience which for me was traumatizing. It only took one experience with losing a child to miscarriage, for me to try and discover my purpose in God allowing me to endure that trial. That phrase occurred in my thoughts again, "Purposeful Wait." All of a sudden the thoughts began to flow uncontrollably. The Lord showed me a group of individuals all waiting on God to fulfill a promise. The people were talking amongst each other and discussing their experiences during the waiting period. The Lord also showed me it was a support group; meaning a place where they could all come to receive emotional and spiritual support during their waiting season. As the thought began to ruminate over and over in my mind, I realized that Purposeful Wait was the title. I grew excited about this idea and could not wait to share it with others.

As the days went by I eagerly thought of different ways to address waiting on God through a Purposeful Wait Support Group. My mind was flooding with ideas and techniques to encourage the people of God. Although everything seemed to be progressing quite rapidly, I humbly accepted the charge that God gave me. I realized that it was nothing but the grace of God that allowed me to endure the pain, waiting, and disappointment only to get me to that particular period in my life. He deserved all the glory and honor for this idea, not me. God was reassuring me of his word, *"And we know that all things work together for good to them that love God, to them who are the called according to his purpose,"* **Romans 8:28**. I was astonished at how God worked such an ugly and painful experience together for my good. I could not believe that something so beautiful other than children could be birthed out of tribulation. What a mighty God I serve!

The time had come for me to share this ministry vision with my pastors, and more importantly parents. I had created a ministry proposal with all the details and vision and mission statements included. I remember sharing the news with my mother and father and them confirming that this type of ministry is so needed today. It felt great that not only did my husband support me, but my mother and father did as well. As I continued to pray and share the vision with my sister and other close friends, I received much encouragement and motivation to follow through. Additionally, the Lord reminded me of a vision he previously gave me of a support group. At the time He did not reveal what type of group it was, however it was evident that the group was needed in order for the participants to be encouraged. Some months later God showed me exactly what type of group it should be, as well as the sort of person it would attract. When God gives you a vision He will direct you in the way you should go concerning that thing. Of course you have to seek Him in order for that vision to thrive and someday be birthed.

For eleven months I had wondered and prayed about the reason for my sorrowful experience. From June 2012 to May of 2013 I had continually cried out to God with the same prayers and more recently a new prayer. It wasn't until May of 2013 when God gave me Purposeful Wait that I truly had peace and understanding about my own encounter. My purpose in pain was finally beginning to make sense. God had allowed me to endure part of the process so that I could effectively and transparently minister to others. I was amazed that God chose me for this assignment, and because He had done so I was not about to take it lightly. My work was just beginning, for now I had a bigger purpose and my suffering had new meaning.

Many people who heard about Purposeful Wait believed that the ministry would just be for encouraging others and empowering them to undergo any waiting process that God allowed in their lives. However, I myself will also be amongst those that will be encouraged. God did not tell me at the time of starting Purposeful Wait that my waiting season was over, but He did show me that He was transitioning me into a new phase of my life.

The Battlefield

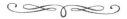

The time finally arrived for me to share publicly the new ministry God placed in my heart. I had prayerfully imagined this day, and was nervously excited to reveal Purposeful Wait. It was Sunday morning and church went on as usual. The Spirit of God was moving throughout praise and worship and I could feel the Holy Spirit near. As I closed my eyes I prayed to God whether or not I should share details of my testimony, when presenting Purposeful Wait. Although I was 100 percent positive that this was a God given vision, in a way I was fearful of what others would think of my loss.

A part of me wanted to tell everybody about my experience and testify as to how He kept me, while another part of my conscience struggled with the idea that everyone would know my private business. For my entire life I had always been a private person when it came to my own personal matters. My confidential tendencies often affected me telling others about what was truly going on in my life. I often blamed this on my profession or should I say "calling" as a Counselor. However, there were a few select friends I shared with every now and then, but mostly matters stayed between me and God.

The moment came for me to speak about Purposeful Wait. As I walked to the front of the church my heart rapidly beat and my body began to perspire; here goes those public speaking symptoms again. I surely believed that God had already delivered me from that fear. Guess I needed to walk in my deliverance! As I opened my mouth to share, the Holy Spirit filled my mouth with the words to say. My personal testimony was amongst those words. I could not believe it; I had overcome my fear to share. The tears expectedly rolled down my eyes swiftly as I recalled the sorrowful feeling of losing my child. Though it had been almost a year, the feeling was still quite potent when I spoke about it. I could tell by the congregation that it was a sad story because some of them were wiping their eyes as well. Towards the end of my speech, I spoke specifically about the birthing of Purposeful Wait. An indescribable joy filled my heart as I gave God all the glory for what He had done. I was beginning to encounter my purpose.

After the service I received many encouraging words from my brothers and sisters in the Lord. This confirmed my peace about sharing my personal story. I knew it was the Holy Spirit that prepared me for that testimony. I later went home in pure joy thanking God for the goodness He was bestowing on my life. I had overcome the enemy with my testimony! *"And they overcame him by the blood of the Lamb, and by the word of their testimony; and they loved not their lives unto death"* **Revelation 12:11**.

That week I continued to rejoice about the things the Lord was doing in my life. I was honored and ecstatic to pursue this new endeavor. My desire to bear children remained, but I had a purpose for my wait! I went to work the whole week excited, until one day another trial entered into my life. I could not believe it. I was in utter shock. I was not even finish rejoicing when the devil TRIED to steal my joy already? Wow! He was really mad! I was persecuted for being concerned about another person, who seemed to be in danger. Nevertheless, I finally realized that this attack was just a tactic of the devil to get me upset and distracted from God's plans. *"Put on the whole armour of God, that ye may be able to stand against the wiles of the devil"* **Ephesians 6:11**. God did see me through that test, but I had to humble myself to allow Him to do that.

When I realized that I was on the battlefield I immediately knew who to call on. Though it was not easy and at times caused me to become emotional, I knew God was on my side. I also was aware that starting a new ministry would most likely be accompanied by some opposition. This battlefield experience reminded me of the significance of Purposeful Wait. Why else would the devil be so mad? After that encounter I was even more confident in God that He would surely see me through in establishing the vision He gave me.

One morning during worship in my home, the Lord gave me a vivid vision of a battlefield. I was on the field and straight before me was an army full of demons and devils large in number. To the side and behind me was a host of angels ready to charge. I began to raise my right hand which held the shield of faith. Though the opposition was great in number, I could see clearly through the enemy's camp. It was a straight pathway that divided the army into two sides. At the end of that long path was a treasure waiting for me. The Lord then gave me the revelation that the path I saw was in fact the journey I was on during my waiting season. The treasure or light shining at the end was my baby. I had to face this battle and destroy the camp in order to receive the manifestation of my treasure. God also revealed that He had already released my firstborn, however I had to be victorious in this battle in order to see the manifestation in the physical. Even though I was excited to be made aware of the treasure, the enemy was vast in number. *"What shall we say to these things? If God be for us, who can be against us?"* **Romans 8:31**.

Release: The Vault Is Opened

My season began to show signs of a shifting. I knew that my promise was soon on its way. It was the very end of May 2013, and every day I thanked God for what He was doing in my life, and waited expectedly on the manifestation. I remember one morning praising the Lord in my home. I was crying out to God not concerned about what my neighbors would think. As I knelt down to pray in my living room, I reminded God of His many promises for my husband and I. I felt the fire of the Holy Spirit and frankly did not care who heard me. I called on the Lord and spoke release into our lives; release spiritually, physically, and financially. Then the Lord showed me another vision in the middle of my prayers. I saw a very large angel standing outside in what looked like a valley. Sitting before the angel there was a very large vault; the type of vault that would take much strength from a human to turn and unlock. Well, the angel went to open the vault and as he turned the wheel, I heard a loud cranking noise followed by the sound of a vault being opened. When the angel opened the door there was an overflow of money and other things that fell out uncontrollably. Then I heard the word "release".

I was so excited about what God had just showed me that I quickly opened my eyes and shared with my husband the wonderful vision. I had already awakened him, that is I already woke him up with my crying and wailing so why not share with him? He instantly rejoiced with me as I spoke to him about what it meant. Although there was a financial release that I saw, I believed in my heart that part of that release was also the manifestation of my children being birthed. There was no doubt that the Lord was nigh and every day after that vision I was in expectation.

It was a few days before my second wedding anniversary and I was uncertain of what I could give my husband for a gift. I jokingly said to myself one day "I wish I could give him something money cannot buy- a child!" The next day I went into the store to purchase an anniversary card for my husband and as I was reading over my choices, the Holy Spirit told me to buy a pregnancy test. Honestly, at first I doubted hearing what I heard but I was obedient and bought one along with my card. When I got into the house I thought about taking the test but also remembered that in early pregnancy it is best to test your urine first thing in the morning because throughout the day urine can be diluted. Even though I knew this I took the test anyway and to my amazement the second line boldly popped up indicating that I was pregnant! On June 25, 2013 I found out I was expecting! I praised and worshiped the Lord with my whole heart! That's how excited I was to know that God had finally blessed us with our hearts desire; our fervent prayers had been answered. Thank you Lord!

The time arrived for me to see my husband later that evening. We were at prayer meeting and the entire time I wanted to whisper in his ear the good news. I could barely hold the surprise. I eagerly wanted to surprise him for our anniversary the next day, but the amount of joy I had could not be shaken. I could not wait to see his response as I told him the wonderful news that the Lord had done it again! So I decided as an anniversary gift I would actually deliver the news to him in a unique way. I placed the pregnancy test in a plastic sandwich bag and placed it in the card which gave a funny hint about him being a father. I had the perfect plan!

Later that night we had to go to a store to pick some things up for our trip to Lancaster, PA the next day. When we finally arrived at the store, I sat Fred down and told him I wanted to give him his anniversary gift right then and there. He begged me to present the gift at home or the next day, but I insisted. I could not hold this exciting secret any longer! I reached in my purse and pulled out the card with the secret inside. He quickly opened up the card and read carefully what it said. When he reached the end of my message in the card, he immediately had a baffled look on his face. Then he turned the small sandwich bag around and stared at the stick. A huge smile came on his face as I congratulated him and said, "You're going to be a daddy"! He jumped out of his seat as we gave God thanks together. Anyone in the store could tell that my husband and I were excited about something! After getting what we had originally come to the store for, we went into the baby section and picked out a beautiful baby blanket to add to our collection of baby items I had already purchased. *"But wilt thou know, O vain man, that faith without works is dead?"* **James 2:20**. I will never ever forget the smile on my husband's face after hearing he was going to be a father; it was indeed priceless.

Twice the Test

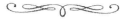

Sunday morning was such an exciting day. I was happy to go into the house of the Lord to honor Him and worship Him for everything that He is and has done in my life. It was my very first Sunday after learning that I was pregnant. It felt great to know that what I had waited and believed God for had finally arrived. I could not wait to share this news with my church family. I knew many of them were praying for my husband and me after they learned about our first loss.

Well, praise and worship that day was so wonderful. I remember closing my eyes and worshipping the Lord in total awe of His goodness and faithfulness. Even throughout the service the Lord spoke to me on many occasions. At the end of service, I made my rounds to several people and greeted them as I made my way to the bathroom. For the last week I was frequently using the bathroom as the pregnancy hormones had affected my bladder. While in the bathroom I went to wipe myself after using the toilet and to my surprise noticed some very light blood on the toilet paper. I flushed it then took a deep breath wondering, "Why am I spotting"? I convinced myself it was nothing but began to pray anyway. I knew I was not losing this child, not after all the waiting and my first experience. God just isn't that type of God.

When I walked back into the sanctuary some negative feelings began to enter my mind. What if I was losing another child? What should I do? The same thing was going to happen again. These are just some of the evil thoughts that ran through my mind. I then walked to my parents and urged them to meet me in their office so that we could pray and refute any attempts of the enemy. My husband and I prayed with my parents in their office. When I left church, I left feeling good and positive.

Once home I used the bathroom again and the bleeding got heavier. I even noticed that my stomach was beginning to cramp really bad. I wiped myself but stayed on the toilet as I sadly thought, "This feels like before when I miscarried my other child." I couldn't help some of these thoughts that were flying into my mind. I quickly tried to distract myself by stating some verses that I learned during the waiting process. I prayed heavily that everything was fine and commanded the devil to leave me and my child alone, in Jesus name! I did not want to tell my husband about the pain because I knew he would worry. I tried to stay strong for the both of us. For the next hour or so I laid on my bed hunched over from the pain. The cramps were really starting to come quicker. I had never been in labor before but the cramps felt like contractions. They were coming more rapidly and heavier. That was it! I was not going to allow this to happen! I stood up and began to pray and speak in the Spirit to my Heavenly Father. As the hour passed, the cramps began to subside and the pain eased up. The next time I used the toilet I noticed large blood clots at the bottom of the bowl. That wasn't a good sign, but I still believed God. However, I knew that I had to call the doctor in the morning.

The following morning I arose to pray and seek the Lord. After spending some time before Him, I called the doctor's office and thoroughly explained to them the symptoms I was having. The nurse told me the best thing to do was just come in to have blood work done. I frustratingly told her about my prior experience and asked if that was all I could do. She answered yes, and then scheduled me to come in that morning for blood work.

Immediately following my appointment at my doctor that same morning, my emotions began to take control of me. I had flashbacks of the first time I was pregnant and going back and forth to the doctors for them to check my HCG (pregnancy hormone) level. Why couldn't this pregnancy just be normal and easy like most people? I did not understand why I was going through what felt like the same trial as before. My faith was being tested drastically and I wondered if my mind would allow me any peace in spite of my concern. I called my mother and told her about the doctor's appointment. I cried to her on the phone about the unfairness of it all. In her own words, she calmly reminded me to trust in the Lord with all my heart and lean not to my own understanding (**see Proverbs 3:5-6**). I could not help but think it was too hard to be calm during this type of situation. I loudly told my mom that God could not allow me to lose another child because He promised me children. My mother prayed with me over the phone, and afterwards I wiped my tears and walked into work asking God for strength.

It was time for me to receive the results from the blood work I had drawn the previous day. This would inevitably determine if I was still pregnant. Blood does not lie. I called the doctor's office and spoke with a nurse. She placed me on hold as she obtained my blood work to read off my HCG and progesterone levels. I waited patiently. When she came back on the line and said, "Your HCG level is 5 and your progesterone test is not back yet. Based on this it looks like you had a very early miscarriage. Anything lower than 5 is considered to be not pregnant." Disappointed, I inquired about another test and told her that I wanted to speak with the doctor. With a gentle tone, she agreed and scheduled me for later that day.

My husband and I attended our scheduled doctor's appointment and met with one of the male doctors at the practice. I was not too enthusiastic about seeing him since I had previously thought he was a bit nonchalant when dealing with me. The doctor explained several things then did a pelvic exam to ensure everything was okay. He also informed us that my period was about to come on and that he did not think I was pregnant, but he was not one hundred percent sure. We were asked several questions about how long we had been trying to conceive. The doctor then briefly discussed fertility options. He talked about in vitro fertilization as well as some infertility tests. I very confidently told him "We will not be going that route." He asked for more details and I told him, "We trust God that He will do it at His time, and will not interfere with that." The doctor did not seem to agree with me, but he also did not oppose my remarks. He mentioned that he did not want to pressure us but simply wanted us to know our options even though he respected our wishes.

Before we left our appointment the doctor told me to come back the following Monday (which was 6 days) to have blood work completed again. He mentioned that by that time my HCG level would probably drop to less than 5, in order to confirm I was no longer pregnant. I held the tears back as we said bye to the doctor and went to the front desk to schedule an appointment to have blood work done. As I reached the area where the receptionists were, I could feel my emotions beginning to rise. The receptionist kindly asked me, "When would you like to come back?" I went to respond and could not get a word out. Instead I cried and mourned in front of the receptionists. My heart was so heavy and there was nothing anyone could do or say that would ease my pain. I was beginning to lose all my hope for the child I was carrying. The receptionist said, "Aw hon don't cry...she really needs a hug." My husband responded by telling the ladies, "It's okay I got her." We left the office and got into the car. During the short ride home the tears rolled down my face until the top of my entire shirt was damp.

Walking into the house my cries became more hysterical. I just let it all out. What I had been holding in for the past few days finally manifested in a way I did not expect. My husband grabbed me and hugged me as I wept in his arms. I apologized to him several times. At that moment I had felt like I caused another miscarriage to happen. The enemy was feeding me ideas and I was giving in to everything that came to mind. What I was trying to avoid finally occurred, I lost control. I was weak and carried so much guilt and shame in my heart. My husband continued to let me cry until he sat me down and said to me, "Babe you have to stop crying." He then started to pray. After he finished he continued to speak life to me and corrected me gently. As I sat there with a flat expression on my face, he told me to believe and reminded me that God has the final say. Well, the Holy Spirit gave him the right words to say because after that I was praying and reading the Word of God.

During prayer early one morning, the Lord spoke to me concerning my ways. He first reminded me of a book I read recently, which describes a woman's testimony about conceiving. In the book, the woman believed God to become pregnant and birth a child. She in fact did conceive, and during her fourth month of pregnancy she miscarried. The woman spoke very clearly about seeking God after she lost her child, and asking Him if there was anything she did to deserve what happened. The Lord responded to her and said that when he finally blessed her with her heart's desire, it almost became an idol to her. She stopped attending church and being faithful as she once was before becoming pregnant. God allowed her to lose that child in order to return her back to her first love-the Lord. Once the Lord reminded me of the book's passage, the Holy Spirit quickly convicted me of my sin. In my mind I did not believe that I had become obsessed with having a child again, but the Lord knew my heart. He saw that I started to get tied up in my thoughts and preoccupied with the idea of pregnancy. The tear ducts in my eyes began to flood as I repented before the Lord and vowed to never allow my desire to bear children to become an idol. Once I finished repenting, I heard a still small voice say, "Your sin made it difficult to trust me." That statement stayed with me for hours until finally the Lord revealed to me exactly what was meant for me to understand. In **Hebrews 11:6,** the Bible reads, *"But without faith it is impossible to please him: for he that cometh to God must believe that he is, and that he is a rewarder of them that diligently seek him."*

Not only was I beginning to preoccupy myself with thoughts of pregnancy, but I was also worried about whether or not this pregnancy would result in a miscarriage. My fixation and worry filled my heart, which made it almost impossible to have faith in God and trust fully in Him. This is why it is imperative to have faith in God because without it we will never be able to cast down every imagination that is not like Him!

Arrival of the Verdict

Monday arrived and it was time for another doctor's visit to get blood work done. My wait for the nurse to call me back seemed to take forever. I remember reading over a few faith verses in my phone, while seated in the waiting room. I ended up going to the receptionist to follow up with my appointment. She then told me that she had cancelled my appointment in the computer by mistake. In a very apologetic tone, she proceeded to tell me it would not be much longer. This was the same receptionist that witnessed my emotional breakdown in the doctor's office the week before. She was definitely being as gentle and apologetic as possible. A few minutes later the nurse called me back and before I knew it I was being pricked for some blood.

The following day I arose from bed and spent some time before the Lord early in the morning. I felt at ease in my spirit at this time, and hoped that through prayer I would remain this way throughout the day.

About three hours later I was packing my lunch for work when I suddenly got the urge to call the doctor's office for my test results from the blood work taken the day prior. After a few minutes on hold, I was connected to a nurse who placed me back on hold in order to fetch my test results. My heart began to beat a little faster as I anticipated the positive results. She came back on the phone about two minutes later and said, "Your HCG (the hormone that detects pregnancy) level indicated that you are not pregnant." She then proceeded to provide an explanation of why she came to this conclusion. I calmly asked her a few questions. She responded then asked me if I was trying to get pregnant. I replied, "Yes." She said, "Well how long have you been trying?" I said "for about one year." I also added some details about my miscarriage a little over a year ago. She then inquired about my desire to discuss fertility options. Although I was not totally for it I replied, "We will talk with the doctor."

Throughout the work day my emotions varied as time passed. When I heard the bad news earlier, immediately a peace had come over me that I had not expected that quickly. However, as the day progressed my thoughts ruminated in my mind, which gave birth to me wondering why this shameful thing happened to me again. The truth of the matter is I was broken. Although I went through the day often smiling and joking with others, deep down inside I was bleeding. Later that night I had attended a church service as my church had a guest speaker. I remember feeling okay as I entered into the sanctuary. In fact, I was able to participate in praise and worship, but the entire time I felt numb inside. The deep rooted emotions and feelings that were lingering inside were not matching up to my affect or facial expressions. I would get up and greet others smiling and hugging them. Little did they know I was aching inside, and hurting with a pain that was indescribable. Even though I truly did not understand what happened and why God allowed me to encounter this trauma again, I was very careful about the words that came out of my mouth. I was sure not to speak anything negative that would cancel my future blessings.

The next morning I awoke to go into my living room and spend some alone time with the Lord. I sang a few psalms then proceeded to pray. As I knelt on the floor I attempted to get a prayer out. I struggled to come up with the right words, so instead I just laid there. My heart was aching so bad that I didn't even know the right words to send up to my Creator. Can you believe that? Although God allowed my situation, I was uneasy about what to say to Him. I had learned from the past not to speak idle words to the Lord, or communicate in a disrespectful manner. I was not going that route. So I just continued to lay there, until I reached for my Bible and began to read about faith and promises. The passages I found blessed my soul; *"So then faith cometh by hearing, and hearing by the word of God,"* **Romans 10:17**.

A Peace of Faith

It would be dishonest to say that I did not experience some negative feelings after learning that the child I once carried was no longer with me. One of the feelings I found it hardest to shake was guilt. For some reason I felt like my faith was not where it needed to be to endure the test again. Although I knew I had faith, I did not exercise it nor access it as much as I should have. I blamed myself for not confessing more of God's Word into my situation at the time. I was so busy praying that I did not speak the words that have power to change any situation.

In **Exodus 23:25-26 (NIV)** the Bible reads, *"Worship the Lord your God, and his blessing will be on your food and water. I will take away sickness from among you, 26 and none will miscarry or be barren in your land. I will give you a full life span."* **Isaiah 55:11,** *"So shall my word be that goeth forth out of my mouth; it shall not return unto me void, but it shall accomplish that which I please, and it shall prosper in the thing whereto I* *sent it."* It is the unadulterated Word of God that can change any situation or circumstance. How do we know this? The Bible is the Word of God meaning, He said it. According to **Isaiah 55:11**, God's Word will do exactly what He said it would do. Sometimes we accept things (curses) in our lives when Christ has already redeemed us from the curse of the law, i.e. *"Christ hath redeemed us from the curse of the law, being made a curse for us: for it is written, Cursed is every one that hangeth on a tree"* **Galatians 3:13**. Therefore, I fault myself in not speaking more of God's pure Word. However, I also know that God can turn every mistake or situation around. He will allow those sorrowful or bad experiences we encounter to work out for our good. *"And we know that all things work together for good to them that love God, to them who are the called according to his purpose"* **Romans 8:28**.

Once the Lord showed me more of His Word and His will for children and offspring, I was better able to understand exactly what I needed to do. I began reading spiritual books regarding pregnancy and childbirth. Some of these tools were the instruments that God used to encourage me to learn more about God's promises concerning children. To my amazement through revelation in His Word, I finally realized that the Word of God was the most significant ingredient to the fulfillment of His promises. For instance, imagine a baker preparing a cake from scratch, but forgetting to include the most important ingredient in the mixture; in this case we can say flour. Well without that flour I am certain the cake will be lacking in the end, if it even bakes at all. This analogy is similar to those believing or waiting on God for something. We can think we are doing the right thing, but ultimately forgetting some key concepts.

The Word of God is needed so much during the waiting process. I cannot fully claim that I left out the Word of God, but I certainly was not using enough of it. Again, if we compare the Word to that key ingredient used in baking, not enough of it will also result in failure. As believers, Christians gain faith through reading the Bible. *"So then faith cometh by hearing, and hearing by the word of God."* **Romans 10:17**. That is why reading, reciting, and hearing the Word of God has increased my faith to believe that He has already blessed my womb, which will bring forth fruit in its due season. After my second miscarriage I felt even more compelled to get deeper in His Word. I knew that it was my faith that would allow the manifestation to occur. As days and weeks passed, I continued to read more and confessed the words into my life.

Yes I was still waiting, but a peace came over me even faster than it did the first time I lost a child. I was excited to realize that although a similar experience occurred, my reaction to this unfortunate happening was not the same. Before, it took me quite a while to be able to accept this particular situation as something God was going to use for my good. However, this time was different. Though some similar feelings initially entered my heart I did not allow them to stay there as long as I did before. I had learned from my first experience and knew it would not benefit me to stay in the "Stupid Place" forever. I can only thank God and give Him glory for His Holy Spirit that comforted me and guided me when I was broken.

No matter the extent of your brokenness, always

remember that God can and will restore. He is an able God, so regardless of the hurt, shame, or emptiness, realize that there is no void that His Spirit cannot fill.

Although I am still waiting on the manifestation of my promise I am truly able to say that I am at peace. My prayer for every reader is that you will experience the peace of God which passeth all understanding (see **Philippians 4:7**). Waiting can certainly be a time of distress; that is if we allow it to be. When we have peace from God we are able to endure whatever process God intended for us to go through. There will be tests, and trials, but I am living proof that one does not have to succumb to the pressures of the enemy and world. Instead one can experience the same peace of faith that God gave me. That's right a peace of faith, not piece of faith. When one has true faith in the God they serve, they will inevitably experience the actual peace of having faith. In other words, there will not be much worrying, doubting, fear, or other negative emotions that may follow sufferings. Instead of those self-defeated emotions there will be joy, peace, and patience. Anyone can wait for certain things to happen in their life, yet it takes one with the mind of Christ to endure a Purposeful Wait. Remember to always ask yourself, which behavior am I practicing?

Purposeful Wait Precepts

Fifteen months ago no one could have told me that my life would be full of tests and challenges concerning having children. Before my husband and I even thought of having kids, we believed like most people that it would come easily and quickly; but it didn't. When this detour to conception and childbirth began, I knew it was no ordinary wait. Nonetheless, during my waiting season God began to deposit in me some truths about truly waiting on Him.

These Purposeful Wait Precepts are Godly standards that the Lord had to instill in me during my process of brokenness. I have learned more in my valley experience than any mountaintop experience could possibly teach me. As I share these principles, I pray that the information blesses you and motivates you to embark on your Purposeful Wait.

Rejoicing with Others vs. Jealousy

After my first experience of losing a child I was angry-angry about my situation, and angry about why others got to keep their children when mine never entered this world. I recall several times asking God why He allowed so many children to be born into this world that people didn't even want, yet when I learned I was pregnant I wanted my child and lost it. The bitterness that filled my heart gave way to something even greater-jealousy. That's right...JEALOUSY! For quite some time I found it hard to rejoice with other people who were expecting children. It was quite pathetic, but my unhappiness and desire to have children so much was beginning to change my character. I had never struggled with jealousy all my life. That was something I always took pride in. I may have struggled with some things, but jealousy was never one of them.

During your season of waiting you will surely

be tested in the area of rejoicing with others. It will almost seem like everyone is being blessed with the one thing you are asking God to do in your own life. It happened to me on a level I would never have imagined. Almost every month I was learning of someone who was now pregnant and expecting a child. In my heart I felt like I was being tortured. Constantly seeing others barely cherish this blessing while I was so busy reaching for it, was truly a battle. It was also hard watching others desire children and finally get blessed, while I was still stuck waiting. For a while, I would literally try to rejoice with them but deep down inside I was not happy.

There were several times when I just cried for hours wondering why God just skipped over me; at least that's what it felt like. I asked God why they were being blessed and I wasn't. What did they do that I didn't do? Why it wasn't me instead of them? These are all questions I asked and at the time did not receive a response. I was tired of hearing how everyone else was birthing children, yet I felt stagnant with no fruit from my womb. It was a miserable state to be in even though I ultimately chose to be there. One day God just began to deal with me about the condition of my heart.

Although I could fool others, God knew every negative feeling that entered my heart. *"The heart is deceitful above all things, and desperately wicked: who can know it?"* **Jeremiah 17:9**. I was so convicted that I had to repent of my jealous and envious feelings. I was fed up and cried out to the Lord in my despair asking Him to change my heart forever. I was tired of feeling the way I did. One moment I was semi-happy for others, then the other minute I was easily triggered into sadness after seeing others wombs being blessed. There in my living room with tears in my eyes, I placed my hand on my heart and asked the Lord to perform heart surgery. When I think of that moment, I know for sure that He was pulling some dirt and other blemishes out of my heart. I cried and wailed as the heartache became heavier, until it slowly began to ease up.

The Lord then spoke to me and told me that my heart and mindset would never be the same. I was so happy I decided to go to the best physician there could possibly be…Jesus! I knew that the surgery would be 100 percent successful because the operator was the healer of all, Jehovah Rapha! It was not until I was honest with God about my jealousy that He delivered me. Although I continued to hear news about others expecting, I could now easily rejoice with them. God was just waiting for me to be honest with myself, because He already saw the condition of my heart.

Often our discontentment with our own circumstances and situations will leave the door open for other negative spirits to begin manifesting in our lives. When we are not pleased with what God has already blessed us with it produces the spirit of an ingrate. Ungratefulness will then lead to jealousy, envy, and covetousness. The Bible reminds us to never give place to the devil, *"and do not give the devil a foothold"* **Ephesians 4:27**. In other words, harboring sin in our hearts and minds gives room for the enemy to step in. We will always see others who appear to have what we want or are where we want to be. The infamous saying goes, "the grass always looks greener on the other side." The devil, being the liar that he is, will tend to make things look better than what they really are. He will create a perfect illusion if we allow him to. If we are so busy wishing we had what others have, we will never get to the promises God has for us.

Instead of being jealous of your brother or sister, begin to ask God how to rejoice with them. **Romans 12:15** reads, *"Rejoice with them that do rejoice, and weep with them that weep."* The key to waiting is rejoicing. Rejoice in your own suffering, and rejoice with others who are rejoicing. God wants us to share in others' joy the same way we would want others to be happy for us. If we really knew the God that we serve, then we would be aware that He is a just God, and not a respecter of persons (see **Romans 2:11**). So begin to rejoice, believing that God is faithful and the same God that blessed others is able to do the same for you!

Thankfulness vs. Complaining

The antidote for complaining is thanksgiving. It is a very simple and easy task that everyone can achieve. All we have to do is think back on the many blessings that God has already given us. That alone is enough to give Him praise and thanks. Even as thanksgiving begins to come out of the mouth, it will start to flow. Before we know it, we will be praising and thanking the Lord for the blessings He has bestowed upon our lives. The Bible says in **1Thessalonians 5:18**, *"In everything give thanks: for this is the will of God in Christ Jesus concerning you."* This passage reminds us that God expects us to give Him thanks regardless of the situation. We could have lost a loved one, yet the Word of God says to give thanks in everything! It does not say give thanks in some things, or even better, give thanks in what you want. Instead the text confirms that the circumstances are God's will concerning us. Even though

God permitted it to occur in our lives and even though the tears may come, we are still to give Him thanks.

I remember having to truly understand that though bad things may happen in our lives, God has allowed it. I recall several times crying hysterically thinking to myself, God do you see all of this that happened to me. Can't you see I'm hurting? At the time I was easily moved by my problems and forgot that yes God saw those tears, and of course He knew what was happening because He allowed it! If we are not careful, our murmuring and complaining can lead to discontentment which then can lead to misery. Despite God's will for our lives, His will is never for us to end up miserable. Those are our own fleshly responses to discomfort. Furthermore, our growing pains should be teaching us how to mature. A mature response to problems and challenges is simply thanksgiving. Thanksgiving does not mean you want matters to remain as they are. However, it does mean that you are accepting God's will for your life at that point.

One of the most bothersome things is to hear a

person constantly complaining about everything! For those around that person it will often annoy them to the point where they confront this complaining individual about their habits. Well imagine how God feels. He is the one who created us and blessed us with life, yet at times we find things to murmur about because they did not go as planned. During the season of wait, there will surely be matters that we hoped would go according to our plan but they didn't. They did not follow our plan because our plans are not God's plans. *"In their hearts humans plan their course; but the Lord establishes their steps"* **Proverbs 16:9 (NIV).** When we are faced with unexpected challenges, the easiest thing to do is complain. Why didn't things just go as planned? What is the point of this detour? I don't have the time or patience for this? All of these statements were things I was telling God or harboring in my heart when obstacles came.

Our flesh will easily allow us to continue with this negative mindset, which is so displeasing to God. Again, the enemy will show us everything that is going wrong to take away from the blessings and faithfulness of God. For example, think about a young child who is complaining and asking his father for more. That father has already given that child what he wanted and more, yet nothing seems to please him. It must grieve the father to see his child constantly complaining about things when he has worked so hard to give his child the best. In like manner, God desires to give us His best, but sometimes we are so stuck on the challenges that we lose focus of our accomplishments through Christ. God already blessed us with a job that we needed, but now that job is not paying enough so every day we go to work complaining.

The next time you are tempted to complain I challenge you to praise and thank God instead. Even when our emotions don't line up with thanksgiving we are obligated to give the Lord thanks. So start to thank the Lord for your conditions and watch how fast He will remind you of how He's blessed you before. That alone is worth thanks!

Faith vs. Fear

It is evident that faith produces miracles, while fear enables defeat. In fact, when believing God to fulfill a promise one will need faith. Without it the journey will inevitably appear never ending. It will almost seem infinite. So how can the waiting season be encouraged by faith? Faith will allow those waiting to be in expectation and hope of receiving the promises of God. Regardless of what is seen or what obstacles occur, faith can determine your outcome!

During the times when I struggled the most with my losses, I always had faith that God would bless us with children. Though my faith was tested several times I knew that sooner or later it would have to happen. When the dark days came, I would cry out to the Lord and ask for His help. I needed His peace to overtake me when my anxiety began to elevate. My worry was never whether or not it would happen, it was just when. To my amazement when the cries went forth, He always allowed me to read a passage or text in the Bible that encouraged me to keep believing and waiting on Him. *"So then faith cometh by hearing, and hearing by the word of God"* **Romans 10:17**. It was God's word that gave me hope and belief that He would do what He said he would; it was that simple. My constant reading of scriptures about faith and children enabled me to have trust in the Lord. I'm not saying it was easy to maintain my faith. Of course when the trials came I was tempted to be fearful; fearful that the struggle would never end, that I would always be facing giants in this area of my life.

Knowing that God was not tempting me gave me a better understanding of my faith. *"Let no man say when he is tempted, I am tempted of God: for God cannot be tempted with evil, neither tempteth he any man:"* **James 1:13**. In other words I knew that the Lord's perfect will was for me to still have faith even when everything looked impossible. Awareness of God's perfect will is much easier than thinking that fear is an acceptable part of the process. Being ignorant of God's perfect will as believers will surely produce fear. It's the reason I had to learn on my own that God's Word is our instruction. As

Coupon is required to redeem offer in store and must be surrendered at time of purchase. To use on Hallmark.com, Crown Rewards number and online code must be used to redeem offer. Offer valid through 12/24/15 at Hallmark Gold Crown stores in the U.S.A. only and at Hallmark.com on a single store/online visit. Limit one $5.00 savings whether in store or online. Valid on the purchase of any seven cards from Hallmark, including Sunrise totaling $5.00 or more. Excludes gift enclosures and packaged and boxed cards. Not valid on gift card purchases or past purchases, Business Greetings Cards, Ink & Main Personalized Greeting Cards, Hallmark Ecard subscriptions or Feeln subscriptions. Not valid on sites or apps other than Hallmark.com. Customer is responsible for any applicable sales tax and shipping and handling. No cash value. Tax not included. This offer is exclusive for you; coupon may not be redistributed. Internet distribution strictly prohibited. No photocopied, photographed, scanned, mechanically or digitally reproduced or altered coupons accepted. Coupon fraud is punishable by law.

Consumer: On Hallmark.com use online code on the front of this coupon at checkout.

Retailers:
1. Scan customer's Crown Rewards card, where applicable. 2. Scan qualifying purchases. 3. Verify consumer has made purchase requirement of seven Hallmark cards totaling $5.00 or more. 4. Scan this offer UPC to deduct $5.00. Non-C.A.S.H. participants mail coupon to Hallmark Fulfillment Center, Promo Code 48226.

© 2015 Hallmark Licensing, LLC

4 00231 63370 9

Use your Crown Rewards card to get this offer. Offer valid 10/1/15 – 12/24/15 at participating Hallmark Gold Crown stores in the U.S.A. only and at Hallmark.com. Void where prohibited. Bonus Points on greeting card purchases apply to any cards from Hallmark including Sunrise. Excludes gift enclosures and packaged and boxed cards, Business Greetings Cards, gift cards, Ink & Main Personalized Greeting Cards, Hallmark Ecard subscriptions and Feeln subscriptions. No cash value. Points will be credited automatically and can be verified online at Hallmark.com/CrownRewards.

Bpll2001014658I7

SAVE $5

when you purchase 7 Hallmark cards

Offer valid through 12/24/15. Details on back.

Bring this in to redeem in store or use online at Hallmark.com
Online code: CR5DCCB7G5-AF6V-4GT3-CGUN-OD2I

CROWN REWARDS

NEW! Member Exclusive

EARN 300 BONUS POINTS
when you buy 3 or more Hallmark cards
EARN 100 BONUS POINTS
for each Hallmark Keepsake Ornament you buy

Valid through 12/24/15. Details on back.

Available in store or online at Hallmark.com

CROWN REWARDS

much as it would be easy to just say "Lord increase my faith," the Lord has already given us the tools to expand our faith; His Holy Word. It is our job to read, study, and ask for revelation. Otherwise, we will be stuck thinking that faith is something we simply ask for, and not take any necessary actions to pursue it. Isn't God's word true? *"But wilt thou know, O vain man, that faith without works is dead?"* **James 2:20**.

So during our waiting season why are we susceptible to fear? When a person decides to wait on the Lord, fear can cause them to become stagnant and discouraged to the point where eventually they just give up and the devil has his way. The enemy's plan is to stop us from getting to our appointed purpose, and if he cannot stop us then he will definitely make efforts to deter us as much as possible. Fear will be the biggest tactic that the enemy will use when we are waiting on God for a miracle. It is the easiest thing that will allow a person to forfeit the race. If we are better aware and mindful of the enemy's tactics then we will be better able to recognize them from afar. *"Put on the full armor of God, so that you can take your stand against the devil's schemes"* **Ephesians 6:11 (NIV).**

During both my first and second miscarriage I became fearful that what the doctors warned me of, may actually be true. At the time, I was not aware of what God truly promised his children regarding offspring. I knew some basic scriptures, but did not have a full understanding as I do now. I allowed fear to enter my heart, and once it entered, it was very difficult to come out of it. As much as I believed I had faith and was not worried, in my heart fear was taking precedence over faith. From my own experience with fear one too many times, I want to encourage you to speak the Word of God and rebuke any spirit of fear that tries to enter your heart because God did not give you that spirit. You want what God gives you, which is a spirit of power, love, and a sound mind **(see 2 Timothy 1:7).**

Peace vs. Worry

Peace is such a significant element to any storm. Despite the natural tendency of a storm to rage, peace will allow one to maintain their calm throughout that rough time. Well, a waiting season for most is just like a storm. Rarely is one enjoying their waiting season due to the discomfort and even negative connotation around waiting. However, regardless of what the wait is for, peace will enable one to still have joy even in the storm. Peace is necessary to waiting on God, because without it one will spend so much time worried and anxious about matters that they cannot change. If anyone lacks peace during their wait they should ask for it. *"And the peace of God, which passeth all understanding, shall keep your hearts and minds through Christ Jesus"* **Philippians 4:7**. This is the type of peace needed in the waiting room, the kind that will transcend all understanding. The human mind is always making efforts to rationalize and understand why things happen the way they do. The truth is, only God Himself knows that.

However, it does not stop our minds from trying to figure matters out. When we have acquired true peace from God, our natural efforts to make sense of situations will disintegrate.

Sometimes when we pray for things we are truly praying for the wrong things. I recall earlier in my wait, having to come to the realization that beyond everything else I needed God's peace. Peace was the only thing that would allow me to rest at night, and stop crying every second of the day. Peace was my gateway to recovery; without it I would have never been able to even write this book. As soon as I began to pray for peace the Lord gave it to me, simple as that. I would be dishonest if I said it was this long exaggerated process. He answered my prayers, and the minute he did I was truly able to move on with my life and not dwell on the sadness and heartache of it all. It doesn't mean I was numb to the situation, but instead, it no longer had a stronghold over my life.

Worry is the exact opposite of peace. It is the very thing that can drive anyone to lose their mind. As mentioned earlier, our minds want to figure out why things happen the way they do. Worry can easily allow us to miss the lessons that God is trying to teach us from this wait. We can be concerned about how long our wait will be, or why we had to wait in the first place. The main problem is that worry cannot only wear on our hearts, but our bodies as well. Before you know it, a person has lost sleep and the ability to focus on other matters. When worry interferes with sleep it's a major red flag. A person wants to go to sleep and rest, but instead their mind is racing and thinking about things they have no control over. As soon as this occurs it's time for serious prayer with the Lord. I have been there, and know firsthand that the Lord is able to deliver. He has no desire for us to worry about the affairs of this world. *"Therefore I tell you, do not worry about your life, what you will eat; or about your body, what you will wear. 23 For life is more than food, and the body more than clothes. 24 Consider the ravens: They do not sow or reap, they have no storeroom or barn; yet God feeds them. And how much more valuable you are than birds! 25 Who of you by worrying can add a single hour to your life? 26 Since you cannot do this very little thing, why do you worry about the rest?"* **Luke 12:22-26 (NIV)**.

Remember, God has called you to peace and not worry. Think about your own life. Have you truly received peace about your wait? If you have, good. Be sure to continue walking in that peace and never return to the anxieties of waiting. Moreover, if you are unsure, determine in your heart now that you want peace, and ask the Lord for it today!

Patience vs. Hastiness

Patience; that infamous word. When I think of patience I think of a difficult process, yet positive outcome. It is difficult to obtain, which means one will have to endure some tests and trials to secure it. Once patience begins to birth forth in people's lives, the fruit will be evident. Patience also known as longsuffering, is a fruit of the Spirit. *22"But the fruit of the Spirit is love, joy, peace, longsuffering, gentleness, goodness, faith, 23 Meekness, temperance: against such there is no law"* **Galatians 5:22-23.**

It is something that we should want to have, but often we do not. Why do we lack patience? Often because in order to obtain patience one will be tested! In other words, fiery trials will come and the wait may seem like forever. It will appear as if the storm keeps coming, when really the Lord is trying to develop some patience in us. *"2 My brethren, count it all joy when ye fall into divers temptations; 3 Knowing this, that the trying of your faith worketh patience. 4 But let patience have her perfect work, that ye may be perfect and entire, wanting nothing"* **James 1:2-4.** Based on this text, we should know that God allows trials in our lives to test our faith and develop patience in us. So when we ask for patience we should automatically assume that some tests will in fact come our way. Waiting on God for something can surely be a test! We just need to be encouraged and believe that God is perfecting Himself in us. Giving us exactly what we want immediately will not develop patience or make us mature. It is when we have to suffer long for Christ that patience and perseverance is perfected.

When we are not patient we tend to want everything to be hasty. However, what we need to understand is that God is not a microwave. These days we seem to believe that everything can be done so quickly. That's what I call a "microwave spirit", which tends to operate under the notion that one will not have to wait and work for anything, but instead will be given what he or she pleases in a short period of time. See, microwaves were created to lessen the wait time on heating up foods. Nowadays we are so spoiled that we have the choice to cook something in the oven (which will take much longer), or pop it in the microwave for a shorter length of time. Everything is done in haste!

When God has a calling on your life, what you may want done quickly just will not happen. I am certain of this because I had to learn the hard way. I originally thought I would not have to wait to have children. I used to imagine that whenever my husband and I were ready, it would happen. After my first loss, I was still not convinced that I would be waiting as long as I have been. Once I made up my mind that I wanted to be a mother I just knew the Lord would answer my prayers with haste. After all, I am faithful, I thought. That meant He was obligated to answer my prayers when I asked. The fact that I believed in my heart this was the correct way of viewing the situation, troubles me today. I was only thinking of myself and what I wanted. I desired instant gratification with no delay! Nevertheless, something began to stir up in the inside when God did not do as I pleased. As much as I would like to say it was the Holy Spirit, it was not. It was my own flesh becoming easily frustrated because I had to wait for something that others did not even have to ask for; I was impatient. I did not plan for a wait, and my hasty spirit collided with God's timing. I remember laughing sometimes asking God "Is this a joke?" I just could not believe that I was having this struggle. The very thought of it would irritate me.

Furthermore, what happens when hastiness has begun to control your wait? It is our responsibility to determine if we want to stay like that. If so, we will spend our entire waiting season rushing through a process that was meant to create patience within us. If not, we need to repent and begin to follow God's steps to honoring His timing.

Courage vs. Despair

Endurance through this faith journey is impossible without courage. In fact, courage is a key characteristic of one who conquers their trials. When the thought of a courageous person comes to mind, we often think of a strong warrior with boldness and zeal. Even the physique of a courageous person is thought to be strong. Well, courage begins in the heart. A person could be of the smallest stature and frail, but be the most courageous individual heard of. As we endure the waiting process we will certainly need courage to help us through the challenges and barriers that may come our way.

Courage will permit inner strength that we know only comes from the Lord. In the book of **Joshua chapter 1 verse 9** reads, *"Have not I commanded thee? Be strong and of a good courage; be not afraid, neither be thou dismayed: for the Lord thy God is with thee withersoever thou goest."* This text reminds us that God commands us to be strong and courageous. It is something that we should want to do while walking this faith journey.

Courage is something I had to ask the Lord to help me with. I realized that my sorrowful experiences had left me emotionally drained at times. During those moments I felt like the weakest Christian ever. Throughout my life people had always labeled me as a strong individual. I would always laugh and think to myself, "I bet they wouldn't think that if they saw me at home during my alone time with God." As much as my face reflected calmness in public at times, my inner man was bleeding and hurting so badly. I did not believe I was courageous at the time, because I honestly felt like I was in despair. The more I cried out to the Lord and sought Him for strength, the more courageous and strong I became. I cannot take any glory for that. The Lord heard me in my affliction and delivered me from my fears. *"1 O Lord God of my salvation, I have cried day and night before thee: 2 Let my prayer come before thee: incline thine ear unto my cry"* **Psalm 88:1-2.**

Whenever our hearts lack courage we are

vulnerable to despair. Often those going through fiery trials and tribulations are faced with the negative feelings of despair. Despair is a very dangerous feeling because it can lead to hopelessness. Hopelessness in turn makes the human mind blind to any possibility of positive outcomes. Once hopelessness has set in, then a suicidal spirit can easily creep in. So many people struggle with what is called suicide ideation- the thought or preoccupation with committing suicide. First they are feeling down, then they are in despair, then before you know it they have a desire to end their life because all hope is gone. The moment we allow our hope to disappear, we open ourselves up to the devil's tricks and need the Lord's deliverance to pull us out. Throughout your waiting season you will have to endure some things and may be tempted to fall into self pity and despair. It may feel as though God has forgotten about you, but we should always remember that *"The Lord is nigh unto them that are of a broken heart; and saveth such as be of a contrite spirit"* **Psalm 34:18**. We cannot allow our feelings to dictate how we act. Because you may feel down or in despair does not mean it is acceptable for you to begin isolating yourself and neglecting social activities. I was guilty of this once myself. The Lord had to rebuke me several times when I would say "I just don't feel like being bothered today." Yes it is okay to have times to yourself and stillness before the Lord. However, when one tends to make it a habit because of their current mood then there is a problem.

Determine today that you will not be in despair about this waiting season. Instead, you will be strong and of good courage. You will be hopeful because God is a God full of hope and endless possibilities. Never exclude yourself from the blessing because of your age or amount of waiting time. Have courage and believe that God is able. *"Now unto him that is able to do exceeding abundantly above all that we ask or think, according to the power that worketh in us,"* **Ephesians 3:20**

Persistence vs. Unfaithfulness

A valuable asset to our waiting period is persistence. When one is waiting on God to fulfill a promise there are some responsibilities of the person enduring the trial. It is our duty to continually pray and seek the Lord for whatever He has promised. Regardless of the length of time we have spent waiting, we are to be consistent in our actions and hearts. Persistence will motivate one to constantly seek the Lord and never give up on God. **Luke 18:18** discusses a widow who consistently sought an unjust judge for vengeance against her enemy. At first that judge failed to grant her request. Nevertheless, the widow did not give up. She continually came to the judge and after bothering him so much he finally granted her desire. The text further justifies how a faithful God will soon vindicate us as we cry out to him day and night. There are a few principles that we could learn from this widow in the

Bible. Had the widow given up on the Judge's ruling, than she possibly would have never received her revenge.

So what would have occurred differently if that widow quit after several attempts? We can assume that either she would have never received revenge, or she would have been waiting even longer for justice. This passage exemplifies the power of persistence. It also allows us to imagine what inconsistence or unfaithfulness may produce. Often times we are waiting on God for something and we may lose heart and want to just give up. Or even if we do not literally give up we may stop praying and seeking God about the matter further believing that God is just not hearing us. Whatever the circumstance, God wants us to be faithful towards Him. We cannot expect to pray once a week and read our Bibles only on Sundays and truly believe that we are faithful to God. In this waiting season we must show ourselves to be faithful to God, and return to our first love. *"Nevertheless I have somewhat against thee, because thou hast left thy first love"* **Revelation 2:4**. Our first priority has to be God. God knows when we are seeking Him just for things as if he is some type of genie.

Do we honestly believe that an omnipresent, omnipotent God can be hoodwinked? Not so! We must be faithful to Him first, and faithfully seek Him for His promises. Unfaithfulness will only leave us stagnant and spiritually immature.

We can delay things in our lives because of our lack of consistency. God wants to see that in spite of our problems and challenges, we're still going to trust and believe in Him while continuing to ask for deliverance in prayer. Are we faithful to him now? If we're not, then what will make things different when we receive His blessings? Choose today if you will be persistent and faithful to God and to prayer.

I had to learn through my own experience that despite the many prayers that went up, I was to keep praying. I have to admit that at first I was not like that persistent widow. I would pray several times for weeks, and then leave it alone for a while because I felt I was too focused on the matter. After my second loss I suddenly felt an eagerness to seek God even more for my children. It almost gave me a push to persevere with prayer, fasting, and studying His Word. I knew that the same God that allowed me to conceive the first and second times was the same God that would enable me to conceive a third time, and to actually carry out that pregnancy full term to delivery. I needed that motivation to see me through. God knows exactly what will encourage us to carry out whatever plan He has for our lives. Interestingly, failure can also motive us to become determined to conquer.

In addition, my second miscarriage inspired me to continue writing this book. I had started to write earlier in the year, but never finished it after writing barely two chapters. Well after another yet painful experience my spirit would not allow me to procrastinate any longer. Those days where I felt my worst, I would write. Writing was part of my healing and deliverance. It was the agent God used to see me through such a difficult time.

Furthermore, the Lord placed it in my heart to share my testimony with others in hope of encouraging them to pursue a Purposeful Wait. I pray that all of my tears and grief will not be in vain. My hope is that this memoir will inspire you to seek God for your ordained purpose in your waiting season. There is purpose to every season in our lives. My detour to conception and childbirth naturally appeared to cause heartache, but most importantly it allowed me to discover more of my purpose in God. I encourage you to follow whatever detour God has allowed in your life. Most of the time our trials and tribulations will somehow become a blessing to others: Whether it be through testimony or example. God knows. *"And they overcame him by the blood of the Lamb, and by the word of their testimony; and they loved not their lives unto the death."* **Revelation 12:11**. Thanks and all glory be to God. He brought me from pain to promise. I have overcome!

About Purposeful Wait

Purposeful Wait is a non-profit faith based support group that meets bi-weekly to discuss what God says about waiting, whether it be for healing, deliverance, a spouse, a job, etc. The support group welcomes both males & females over the age of 18 who are eager to fellowship with others who are learning how to positively endure the process of waiting. Support Groups entail a biblical based message, testimonial time, and an open forum.

Our Mission: Seeking to empower others to find their

Godly ordained purpose during their season of wait.

Our Vision: We strive to provide ongoing emotional and spiritual support to individuals who are waiting on God to perform miracles in their lives, based on God's irrefutable promises.

For more information about Purposeful Wait support group and speaking engagements for Rebecca Rush, please contact: purposefulwait@gmail.com or visit our website at www.purposefulwait.com

Made in the USA
Charleston, SC
29 April 2014